TRAVELING WITH TANGERINES

Refreshing Biblical Truth for Women Journeying Through Family Life

BARBARA CRIDER

Woman's Missionary Union
Birmingham, Alabama

Woman's Missionary Union
P. O. Box 830010
Birmingham, Alabama 35283-0010

© 1996 by Woman's Missionary Union
All rights reserved. First printing 1996
Printed in the United States of America

Dewey Decimal Classification: 248.843
Subject Headings: WOMEN—BIBLICAL TEACHING
     CHRISTIAN LIFE—WOMEN
     FAMILY LIFE—BIBLICAL TEACHING
     WOMEN ON MISSION (WMU)—
     HANDBOOKS, MANUALS, ETC.

All Scripture quotations are from the *New Revised Standard Version of the Bible*, Copyright © 1989 by the Division of Christian Education of the National Council of the Churches of Christ in the USA. Used by permission. All rights reserved.

Cover design by Barry Graham

ISBN: 1-56309-166-6
W964103•0696•5M1

Contents

"We are setting out for the place of which the Lord said, 'I will give it to you'; come with us, and we will treat you well; for the Lord has promised good to Israel"
(Num. 10:29b).

Chapter 1: For the Abused 1

Chapter 2: For the Career Woman 5

Chapter 3: For the Family on Mission 9

Chapter 4: For the Grieving 13

Chapter 5: For the Money Manager 17

Chapter 6: For the Afflicted 23

Chapter 7: For the Lonely 28

Chapter 8: For the Busy Mother 32

Chapter 9: For the Rejected 37

Chapter 10: For the Blended Family 41

Chapter 11: For the Communicator 46

Chapter 12: For the Forgiven 52

Tangerines for All 58

Preface

During the 25 years we spent as missionaries in Spain, we logged many miles on bumpy roads and modern superhighways with two and then three children. As we rolled along, cold in winter and parched in summer with the hot breeze in our faces, snacks became a way to break the monotony, refresh the body, and entertain the occupants of the backseat. We soon learned that tangerines are the perfect snack for a road trip—lightweight, they provide juice for the thirsty, something to chew for the hungry, and, no matter how soiled the outside, the meat inside is always clean and ready to eat. Such neat packaging!

In our Christian life, we are all on a journey. We know our goal, but oftentimes the trip is not as smooth as we expected. Sometimes we have trouble understanding the road map, or react with impatience to the detour sign.

Life's pilgrimage is seldom straight, especially for a Christian who is to be ever listening for the "still small voice." We must be ready to stop by the wayside to wipe a runny nose, or to take an unaccustomed path to talk with a "woman at a well." Tiredness will beset us, even as it did our Lord (John 4:6); and we, too, will need to stop for refreshment.

This book seeks to offer that needed renewal of spirit for the weary pilgrim in the form of "tangerines." Each chapter includes a vignette that is similar to **The Bright Orange Skin** of the fruit. It is what we see, the outward action that attracts our attention. Just as a tangerine must be peeled to get at the fruit, so we must probe beyond the obvious to arrive at the fruit that sustains these real flesh-and-blood women. **Beneath the Peel** will lead the reader to an examination of pertinent biblical truths.

The brief stories included are only a sampling of the great abundance to be found, experiences of seemingly ordinary women who have discovered the extraordinary life that Jesus Christ offers.

As you peel back the skin of these studies, I hope you will find fruit to sustain you as women leaning on Christ, and which you can offer to others with the hope of new life in Christ.

Barbara W. Crider

CHAPTER 1

For the Abused

"God is our refuge and strength, a very present help in trouble" (Psalm 46:1).

The Bright Orange Skin

A survey of two randomly-selected classes at a Christian university revealed that 39 percent of the students were or had been in an abusive dating relationship. By any criteria, these would be considered privileged young adults, most of them coming from homes financially able to pay for private higher education and with parents who value the Christian atmosphere and teaching. Yet, the percentage of abusiveness experienced by that select group exceeded the national average of 28 percent.

Studies across the nation have shown that dating violence and abusiveness in the home are at alarming levels. Some episodes, of course, can be related to substance abuse, of either alcohol or addictive drugs. Martha's problems came from both. She hoped things would get better when she began attending church with her family, but her husband could not shake his drug habits and the physical abuse returned. Desperate for a change, Martha opted to leave her husband in order to remove her children from that environment. Now, she worries that it was too late for her older sons.

Rafaela was more fortunate. She and her husband both had good jobs and a couple of children, but with financial security and money in his pockets, Juan began to find pleasures elsewhere. Unfaithful to his wife, he blamed her as his love changed to hate—hate that found expression through abuse. One night, after he had knocked her across the room, he suddenly realized what had happened to them and their lost dream of happiness. He began searching for a way to change, and, in that search, he found God.

Both Juan and his wife became Christians, and the difference was dramatic. The foul language and curses that had flowed so freely from his lips disappeared. The cigarettes that had been a part of his existence for years were now repulsive to him. But the biggest difference of all was seen in his relationship with his wife. God took away the hatefulness and replaced it with love and appreciation. With the return of love, the abuse ceased and faithfulness was restored to the home.

Every abused woman must long for the miracle that Rafaela experienced as God so wondrously changed her husband. Many devoted wives are praying daily for their husband's conversion, and for the home life for which they long. It would be wonderful if all of their prayers could result in a transformation such as Juan experienced, but we know that will not be the case as long as men continue to harden their hearts. What hope is there, then, for women like Martha?

Beneath the Peel

The Bible speaks to this issue by giving us the example of Hagar. Hagar? Wasn't she the mother of Abraham's son? Was the great Hebrew patriarch, a man widely known for his faith, a woman beater? No, but Hagar was, nevertheless, an abused person because she was used.

> **Read the story of Hagar in Genesis 16.**

In all fairness to Abraham, it must be pointed out that the idea of using Hagar to produce a male heir came from his wife Sarai (her name was later changed to Sarah, Gen. 17:15) and not from him. While the idea of willingly giving your maid to your husband as a lover is completely foreign to the mind of a modern American woman, it was a rather common practice in Sarai and Abraham's day. It is even written into ancient Assyrian marriage contracts that have survived to this day, and is a part of the well-known Code of Hammurabi. The absence of a male heir was a serious problem, and the law stated that a barren woman could have children through her maidservant, and that the son born from such an arrangement would be considered a legitimate heir.

At this point, the tangerine looked great on the outside. Sarai's plan worked; Hagar became pregnant. However, the inside was threatened by sourness when Hagar, reveling in her elevated state as the mother-to-be of the future heir, began to despise her mistress.

Alone, pregnant, and a slave, Hagar's situation must have seemed desperate to her. While she did not know which way to turn, God sought her out and ministered to her. The charge she was given was not an easy one.

> **Read Genesis 16:4-6. How did Sarai react to Hagar's pregnancy and attitude?**
>
> **What do you think of her reaction?**
>
> **How did Hagar react to Sarai's treatment of her?**

She bore her son, and the name he was given was a statement of her experience in the wilderness: Ishmael, "God hears." Years later, when the rite of circumcision was established as a sign of faith for male believers in the one true God, Ishmael was among the first, if not the first, on whom it was practiced (Gen. 17:24-26).

4   Traveling with Tangerines

> **Read Genesis 16:7-10. What did God tell Hagar to do?**
>
> **Why do you think this was hard for her?**

Hagar and Sarah (her name now changed by God) apparently learned to coexist in peace for a number of years, but after Sarah's son Isaac was born, she determined that the son of a slave would never share her son's inheritance. Even though Abraham deeply loved his firstborn, he once more, after being comforted by God, gave in to his wife's bidding. Hagar and Ishmael were sent away with only a little food and water (Gen. 21:1-14).

The scene which followed in the desert after their supplies were exhausted is a touching one as a tearful Hagar placed her son under a bush and then withdrew a distance because she could not bear to see him die.

> **Read Genesis 21:15-21. What does Hagar do after leaving her son to die?**

The loving care that God showed Hagar shines as a tender reminder to any abused or mistreated woman. The angel God sends today may be a neighbor, a concerned Sunday School teacher, or a caregiver in a shelter. It is most important for a woman in an abusive situation to realize that she does not have to continue to suffer alone, to hide her shame. Help is available, and she should seek it, for herself, for the sake of her children, and even for her abuser, if possible. Our God offers love freely to all and expects His followers to demonstrate the same love in reaching out to those in need.

> **Read Genesis 21:15-21 again. What does God do? What prompts God to act?**

CHAPTER 2

For the Career Woman

"May the Lord give strength to his people!" (Psalm 29:11a).

The Bright Orange Skin

She gets up while it is dark to provide food for all in her household. She spins thread, weaves cloth, and sews fine garments for her family. Knowledgeable of the market, she profits by trading and buys land and plants vineyards with her earnings. She helps the poor, works hard (Her light is on all night!), and builds a nest egg for the future.

Wow! Talk about Super Woman! The desire to do it all while still being an outstanding wife and mother is not a product of women's liberation after all. A comparison with that wife described by the writer of Proverbs (chapter 31) will easily shake any modern woman who thinks she is doing a pretty good job of running the daily circus.

But the truth is, we yearn to be like her: competent, respected, loved by our children, and praised by our husbands and families. We long to "speak with wisdom" as she did.

As a group, women are better educated than ever before,

6 Traveling with Tangerines

and there is both internal and external pressure not to "waste" that education. Superbly manage a family and a career at the same time? Of course we can! We are "can-do" women.

Rebecca knew exactly what she wanted—to live in what Northeasterners call "the City" and be a lawyer for a large New York firm. At 25, she had achieved her goals, along with a husband and a six-figure salary that went with the territory. Life was exciting. Then, Charlotte was born. Going to work ceased to be as attractive when it meant leaving her daughter at home. After a year of being tugged in opposing directions, Rebecca made a major life change to devote her energies to being a mother.

The Teacher wrote in Ecclesiastes 3:2 that, just as there is "a time to be born," so there is "a time to plant." Surely the time for planting values and spiritual teaching, for establishing bonds of caring love, for guiding an awakening curiosity is when a child is young. Rebecca chose one career over another. Not all women have that choice—not in today's society.

How can a single mom, for example, balance work and caring for her children? Most of the time, she is left to cope with the situation on her own, with no time off, no support system, and often little or no help with expenses. She finds little sympathy either in society as a whole or in the church. Yet, the pressures to be the perfect mother of perfect children remain strong even when one cannot afford to neglect her career.

These are not just the problems of women with children either. Single women and married women without children also struggle with balancing career and family. In many cases, married siblings look to the unmarried female of the family to care for their aging parents. Many married women without children have to work for financial reasons. They may want children, but wonder how they can afford to have children with the costs of child care so high, added to the fact that they are barely getting by without children.

Women, whether married or single, with or without children, will always have to struggle to maintain a balance between working and caring for their families.

Beneath the Peel

We do have some biblical examples of women with careers. Some are called by God to their task.

It is interesting that Paul's first European convert was a businesswoman—Lydia. Surely, Lydia's work provided many contacts with whom she could share her newfound faith.

> **Read Exodus 15:20 and Judges 4-5. Who were the career women mentioned in these passages?**
>
> **What careers did God choose them to tackle?**
>
> **Were these roles typically assigned to women?**
>
> **Why do you think God chose these women?**

Another early Christian who viewed her career as an opportunity to serve God was Priscilla. She and her husband were refugees from Rome when Paul first met them.

These early Christian women understood clearly that they were to serve God through their careers, not in spite of them.

Becky found that she had to work, but more than that she felt called to her job as a teacher. Though at times she was attacked by feelings of guilt for not being with her own children, she felt that God had placed her

> **Read Acts 16:13-15,40. Who was Lydia?**
>
> **What did she do for a living?**
>
> **What role might her job have played in the spread of the gospel?**

as a teacher to reach many more children who did not know Christ.

> **Read Acts 18.**

To a woman who shares the biblical concept of honorable work as being holy unto God, her career becomes a key to opening ever-widening concentric circles of concern. She knows she must guard carefully the words she uses, her reactions to a rude supervisor or customer, and even her expressions if she is to present Christ in the marketplace. To do so—even on days when she would really have preferred to stay in bed—she

---

What was Priscilla's trade?

How were Priscilla and her husband able to use their careers for missions?

How might you use your career to do missions?

---

must be a woman of prayer. Just as the freshness and goodness of a tangerine is savored more when one is thirsty, so it is at this point that a woman savors the power and holiness of the Heavenly Father. The strength she needs is beyond her—it is a superhuman strength, a holy strength . . . a strength that the Father stands eager to give.

CHAPTER 3

For the Family on Mission

"Tell your children of it, and let your children tell their children, and their children another generation" (Joel 1:3).

The Bright Orange Skin

"Paul Duke, a pastor in St. Louis, Missouri, charges that the family can be the most dangerous of all human institutions when its loyalties are turned inward. He says we've been led to focus *on* the family, rather than finding a focus *of* the family."

This quotation from her regular column in *The Birmingham News* expresses a conviction Alabama novelist Vicki Covington puts into action as a mother. She, her writer/professor husband Dennis Covington, and their daughters Ashley and Laura found their focus in missions outreach through their church.

It began when seven-year-old Zahra from Iran began attending Vacation Bible School one summer. Both Zahra and her brother were hearing-impaired. After Bible school ended, Dennis continued to pick the children up for Sunday School. In order to communicate with them, Vicki enrolled in a sign language class and would then go home and teach her children what she had learned. When Ashley, also seven at the time, signed "I love you" to Zahra and she responded with the same sign, Ashley leaped for joy. Zahra realized that someone cared enough about her to learn to communicate with her; Ashley experienced the joy of ministry. Not long after that experience, Ashley trusted Christ as her Savior and was baptized.

When a group from the church made a missions trip to Kentucky, Dennis and Vicki decided to take their small daughters. Their participation in Backyard Bible Clubs and other activities reaffirmed their involvement as a family in missions outreach.

Fear of AIDS, now a leading cause of death for young adults in our country, is so strong that schools where HIV-positive children attend have been boycotted. Despite the fear surrounding AIDS, the Covingtons, including Ashley, aged eight, and Laura, six, were dedicated in front of the congregation as members of their church's AIDS Care Team. As a family, they have a week each month during which they are responsible for men who live in a house for people with AIDS. At times, they take those they care for to a movie or shopping; other times, they take them food or help them with the yard work. This personal involvement through a ministry of friendship is, in Vicki's words, "a way to pierce through what we think of as an issue and turn it into people with needs." In the process, the girls have learned many of the hard facts of the disease, but they also learned to better understand the work of the Holy Spirit. Barriers fell and people who were once ostracized by the church are now attending worship services. And prayer has become a natural part of life for two young girls as their family prays for those to whom they minister.

Is this not teaching at its best, by both word and example? The best of tangerines, with the inside fulfilling the promise of the outside?

Beneath the Peel

By making ministry a family affair, Vicki has resolved what is a conflict for many women—the tug between unavoidable family responsibilities and the desire to "do the Lord's work."

Basic to this struggle is the mistaken idea that the only way one can serve God is by doing church-related activities. A woman can sing in the choir, be faithful in attending Women on Mission events, cook for youth socials, send cards to church members who are shut-ins, and teach Sunday School. The more often a woman is somewhere in the church building, the more she fits the modern concept of a dedicated Christian woman. While all these activities are good in and of themselves, if they cause a woman to neglect her family is she being the type servant God desires?

Paul warns that "Whoever does not provide for relatives, and especially for family members, has denied the faith and is worse than an unbeliever" (1 Tim. 5:8). In context, Paul refers to the believer's responsibility to care for helpless widows, but this verse clearly extends the obligation to all family members. Both their material and spiritual needs are to form a part of our service to God as Christians.

The challenge, therefore, is not whether to serve God even if it means ignoring our families but rather to serve Him with our families. The determined declaration of Joshua so many centuries ago should be that of the modern Christian woman. Children who see their parents respond in love to the needs of others will be more likely to discuss their own problems and spiritual quest with Mom and Dad.

> **Read Joshua 24:15b.**

The Apostle Paul's spiritual son was Timothy. Even though his father was a Greek and, it is assumed, a nonbeliever, Timothy had been carefully taught the Scriptures. It is not known if Timothy was converted during Paul's first visit to Lystra or later, but by the time he arrived for his second visit,

> **Read 2 Timothy 1:5 and 3:14-15. Who was responsible for teaching Timothy the Scriptures?**

> **Read Acts 16:1-2. Why do you think Timothy rose so quickly in the esteem of Paul and other Christians?**

Timothy was highly regarded by other Christians in the town (Acts 16:1-2).

The influence of a mother is evident in the life of another of Paul's companions, John Mark. He was the son of a woman named Mary, and it was in her home that the disciples commonly met for prayer in Jerusalem. When Peter was released from prison, he immediately went to her home where he knew the others would be gathered (Acts 12:12). Some Bible scholars have even surmised that it was in her upper room that the Last Supper was held, and that the mysterious young man who was following Jesus the night of His arrest was Mark (Mark 14:51-52).

> **Read Proverbs 22:6. What do you think this passage means?**

The Bible indicates that Mary's ministry was one of hospitality and prayer, and that her son was strongly influenced by her faith and by those with whom he came in contact through her willingness to serve her Lord. Through the centuries, countless other children have sat around the table with great ministers of the faith who were invited into the home to share a meal prepared by a woman practicing the ministry of hospitality. It is yet another way to involve the entire family in Christian service . . . opening our homes to others, using our homes and our means as opportunities to share love in Christ's name.

> **Are you currently involved in missions?**
> **Were either one of your parents involved in missions?**
>
> **How do you think their involvement or the lack of it influenced you?**

CHAPTER 4

For the Grieving

"Blessed are those who mourn, for they will be comforted" (Matt. 5:4).

The Bright Orange Skin

The radiant face beneath a full head of snow-white hair in the choir catches the eye. Looking on this image of serenity, no one would ever imagine that Viola Mix had known deep suffering—the heartrending suffering that only a parent who has lost a child can know.

Her cherished daughter was a young bride of only 21 when cancer struck the nerves of her spinal column, leaving her bedridden. Unable to leave two young teenaged children, Viola and her husband decided to take their daughter home so the family could better care for her. It was in that familiar setting, so filled with happier memories, that Mary Lynn, with her husband at her side, left the sufferings of this life early one Sunday morning.

Barbara Dunn's loss was without warning. It was a lovely Florida Thanksgiving Day when her 14-year-old son, Tommy, went for a ride on his moped. The traffic light at the corner of Highway 98 and Michigan Avenue was not working properly, and neither the car nor the moped stopped in time. Although the driver of the car was a doctor who sought to administer first aid on the way to the hospital, nothing could be done to save Tommy's life.

The pastor was at their house immediately upon hearing of the accident, and the support of the entire church family was crucial in getting them through those early days. Barbara says: "I've lost my father and my husband and Tommy. There's something about losing a child that really tears your heart out, and I'll never understand how a non-Christian could survive it. . . . I recall that a mother who'd lost her son a few years earlier told me that it never got any easier. Thank God she was wrong, although there will always be a void because of not being able to see Tommy grow up."

Once more, God was able to bring comfort out of tragedy, true to His promise to those who believe in Him. Among the blessings the family received was getting to know the family of the man who had collided with Tommy. His daughter, Kay, and Barbara's daughter, Janie, even became best friends and remained so until Kay's death of bone cancer at age 20. Even after more than 30 years, the families continue to share a special bond.

> Read John 14:15-27.

Beneath the Peel

The Bible does not lack examples of parents who suffered the loss of a child, beginning with Adam and Eve who, in reality, lost two sons. Abel was murdered by a jealous brother who was later banished from his home. Nothing is said of Adam and Eve's reactions, but it is not difficult to imagine the deep sorrow they surely felt.

Jacob refused to be comforted when told his beloved Joseph had been killed (Gen. 37:35), and Job

> Read 2 Samuel 12:1-25, 13:23-37, and 18:1-19:4. What were the causes of David's mourning in each instance?

experienced deep mourning after losing all his children.

Even with all his worldly success and his devotion to God, David was not spared a father's greatest heartbreak. The words spoken by David after he learned of Absalom's

> Have you ever experienced grief? The death of a family member? Describe how you felt.
>
> When did you begin to feel some comfort? What comforted you?

death have been called one of the most moving expressions of a father's love for his son in all literature: "O my son Absalom, my son, my son Absalom! Would I had died instead of you, O Absalom, my son, my son!" (2 Sam. 18:33b).

David's grief was so deep that the king was incapable of governing. His love for his son became a threat not only to him but to the nation. It took Joab to convince him to go back to work and to get on with life.

> Read Isaiah 61, focusing on verses 2-3. What did God send His servant to do for those who mourn and grieve?

In our own grief, the fate of a nation may not be at stake, but more than one marriage has been known to have ended because either the husband or the wife could not deal with grief in a healthy manner. Excessive mourning can still destroy. All of life can become like a bitter tangerine, the pleasant taste replaced by a lingering sourness.

Both Viola and Barbara testify to the strength and comfort brought by Christian friends as they sought to deal with the grief process. A friend wrote Viola that Mary Lynn had finally reached the goal toward which her parents had been pointing her all her short life. Through their tears, they agreed. Knowing that heaven was a reality for their daughter enabled them to be thankful in the midst of sorrow.

As Barbara fought to refocus her life, she began to do some volunteer work in the church office and in the process discovered

> **Read the last part of Isaiah 61:3 again. What do you think this verse means? Does this verse infer a reason for grief and the comfort of God that follows?**

a career. She later became church secretary, a job she held for over 15 years. Staying actively involved in helping others, whether typing the church bulletin or delivering home-baked bread as a tangible means of sharing love, helped Barbara reach beyond mourning to live in a manner that continues to touch and bless others.

While the Bible clearly shows by human examples and by word that a time for mourning is necessary, it also teaches that God enables His children to continue to live in a triumphant, even joyful, manner. Mary's sorrow in seeing her son die on the cross was transformed into everlasting joy by the resurrection. This same experience can be that of any Christian. John 14 is often read at funeral services because of the comfort and the hope those words of Christ offer. He has left us a Comforter, the Holy Spirit, to give us the peace we cannot find alone. "For just as the sufferings of Christ are abundant for us, so also our consolation is abundant through Christ" (2 Cor. 1:5).

> **Read Ecclesiastes 3:1-14.**

CHAPTER 5

For the Money Manager

"Keep your lives free from the love of money and be content with what you have" (Heb. 13:5).

The Bright Orange Skin

"Prepare to be a widow!" Dorothy Funderburg repeatedly gave this advice to her young students at Samford University for a good reason. Most married women will be widows. It is a fact of life that women, on average, outlive men, and Professor Funderburg felt strongly that women need to be prepared for that eventuality.

Too many are not. Too many married women leave the family finances in the hands of their husbands without a clue as to their real financial circumstances until suddenly they find it all in their hands. Too many single women depend on their fathers for financial help, and then one day find that they have to manage on their own.

These are extremes, of course. On the other end of the financial spectrum are those women whose husbands leave the management of their finances entirely up to them, or whose fathers give them open-ended checking or credit.

Then, there are those two-income families. Is each to decide individually how his/her money will be spent, or are the funds pooled?

Money management is a common source of stress for many families. Dolores Curran, author of *Stress and the Healthy Family*, found that married men, married women, and single mothers all named "economics/finances/budgeting" as the situation causing the most stress in their family life.

Although most people think the solution to their financial problems is more money, experience disproves this theory. Rich families as well as poor argue over how the money will be spent. A recent survey of people who had won million-dollar lotteries or sweepstakes revealed that everyone in the group was happier when they had less money. The problem is not the quantity of money flowing in, but rather its administration, which generally reflects attitudes toward money.

Beneath the Peel

What should be the attitude of a Christian toward money? Were the hermits of ancient Christianity on the right track when they renounced all possessions and fled to live alone in the hills?

The Bible certainly warns us of the conflicts money can cause. A careful reading of 1 Timothy 6:10 reveals the root of the problem. In the more than

> **Read Matthew 6:19-24. In your own words, what does this passage say?**

700 verses in the Bible that speak of attitudes toward possessions,

> **Read 1 Timothy 6:3-10. Summarize the meaning of the passage.**

including money, we find guidelines for maintaining the physical and the spiritual in proper order. If God's priorities are followed, Christians can know freedom as they cease being slaves to the dollar and make it their servant instead.

> **Read Deuteronomy 10:14 and Psalm 24:1. What biblical principle do they teach?**

The Bible teaches that while everything belongs to God, God has given human beings the responsibility of administration. Abraham, a very wealthy man for his time, recognized and accepted this responsibility. Cognizant that all he possessed really belonged to God, he practiced a stewardship that included returning to God a tenth of all the goods he had (Gen. 14:20). His descendants continued this practice, and incorporated the tithe into the laws that governed Israel (Lev. 27:3-34).

Many confuse the tithe with stewardship, but tithes and offerings are only tangible expressions of the acknowledgment of God as the true owner of all one's possessions. Jesus taught a complete stewardship of life.

Julio and Angelina have made this concept the basis of their family finances. When still newly married, Julio underwent heart surgery for a valve replacement that left the couple without any income for a number of months. During that time, he happened to find 50 cents lying on the street. Joyfully, he scooped it up and into his pocket. That Sunday, the same 50 cents was placed in the offering plate with thanksgiving to God for providing them with something to give.

In both times of scarcity and times when it was a little easier to buy the food they needed, they have always found a way to make the soup and the rice stretch to include others around the table. The doors to their home are open, as are their hearts. A complete stewardship of life means a willingness to share what one has for God's glory.

It is also a natural consequence of accepting God's ownership of all we claim to have. If we ourselves are God's, how can we maintain a closed fist around what He gives?

> **Read Matthew 5:13.**

Generosity is one way Christians can be the salt of the earth. Each area of life can be a testimony to our faith, or it can be a barrier. The way we administer money is certainly an area open to inspection by others.

A businessman talks of a past minister. He owed him money when he left town and has not bothered to send a payment since. A banker watches as a fellow church member collects the offering and considers dropping a note in the offering plate to ask him about the house payment he has failed to make for several months now.

Failures of Christians to take financial obligations such as these seriously present formidable stumbling blocks for others. If Christians are to fulfill Christ's desire that we be salt in this society, then we must carefully guard our use of money.

This includes, also, wise planning for the future. Jesus told a parable about three servants who received sums of money from their master. The example of this parable illustrates that being a good steward includes seeking to improve upon what

> **Read Matthew 25:14-30. Summarize the parable. What is the point of the parable?**

the Lord gives us. We may have only a handful of seeds, but, carefully planted and cultivated, they could produce an orchard of tangerines.

The wise use of what God gives requires that we at least try to plan for the future. This involves gathering adequate information about investments and being willing to make minor sacrifices now in hopes of not being forced to make more in our old age. This is important if you do not wish to burden your children financially later in life, or if you are single and must of necessity make provisions for those years when you can no longer work.

In all of money management, a Christian is to be guided by a higher purpose than the accumulation of riches.

> Read 1 John 3:16-20. What does this passage say about material possessions and the love of God?

If one is to seek to manage money wisely according to concepts given in the Bible, a plan is necessary. A family budget helps to control expenses and keeps them within bounds of income, but a family management plan involves much more.

If it is to work, a financial plan must have the support of the entire family. First of all, they must agree on goals. When the children are young, of course, parents alone are involved, but efforts should be made to gradually include them as they get older and can assume responsibilities.

It is in trying to set common goals that disagreements often flare. Mother wants a new couch, Caroline wants ballet lessons, Johnny has his eye on a new mountain bike, and Dad has a new car all picked out. It is clear that not every wish can be granted on a set income. Whose wins out? Who decides? Is a new car just a selfish wish or is it a sound investment? Clear-cut answers often are not easily found.

Overall, long-term goals need to be set before immediate needs (wants) are addressed. Financial plans should take into consideration the distant future as well as present circumstances.

The latter, of course, needs to be carefully analyzed. This involves a careful listing of all income as well as one of expenses. Fixed expenses are those that cannot be altered and must be paid on a regular basis. They are a primary obligation. Variable expenses can be examined on the basis of priority. Food, for example, is a variable expense of high priority. We must have it in order to live, but, is there a way to still eat well while paying less? Other variable expenses should be examined in a similar fashion.

The proper time to look at alternatives is when the figures are down on paper. Once the present financial situation and both present and future needs are evident, it may be necessary to adjust some of the goals. Perhaps that Caribbean cruise will have to wait until another year, or a used car rather than a shiny new one will have to be purchased. Decisions like these can be tough, but they are made easier when based on hard facts rather than emotions.

This is the time, too, for selfish desires to give way to the overall good of the family. The sense of unity of purpose must win over personal preferences.

Once a financial plan is designed based on what are considered the best alternatives, the time arrives for putting the plan in practice. This calls for restraint on the part of all. Perhaps it may involve drastic changes in lifestyle which will not be easy.

The plan, however, must not be considered to be infallible and ironclad, for then the paper and the money it represents will rule the steward. All budgets need a certain elasticity, and all financial plans need to be revised periodically. Needs change, and emergencies occur. Plans and money are meant to serve us and not the other way around.

No matter the personal or family income, it will be better used if we seek to apply biblical principles. The use of our money is an integral part of our Christian testimony, whether positive or negative. If it is to be seen as evidence of a strong Christian faith, it must reflect a conviction that we and all we have belong to the Lord. The result will be generosity. Our use of money will also reveal our conviction He has made us caretakers for a time. The result will be careful planning as we should take that responsibility seriously.

> **Read Hebrews 13:5. What does it mean and how will it affect your life?**

CHAPTER 6

For the Afflicted

"O come, let us worship and bow down, let us kneel before the Lord, our Maker! For he is our God, and we are the people of his pasture, and the sheep of his hand" (Psalm 95:6-7).

The Bright Orange Skin

As Discipleship Training at Brent Baptist Church was ending, the lightning outside the window brightened the sky as the storm grew more intense. Just as the class was leaving the upstairs room, the lights went out. They began groping their way in the dark down the staircase that led to the sanctuary. In an instant, the tornado struck and Fay Dowdle's life was changed forever.

Flying debris hit Fay. Her left leg was bleeding profusely. A nurse in the congregation applied a tourniquet to control the loss of blood, but not before Fay lost consciousness. The parking lot was a mass of destroyed cars. Finally one was found that could run, although the windows were blown out and the rain poured in. The driver headed for the hospital in Marion, where Fay was to remain with her leg in traction for the next six months. During much of that time, she was so sedated she was not very aware of her surroundings. To the family, she looked as if she were slowly but surely dying.

After a year of hospitalization, the decision was made to amputate the leg above the knee. Once a very active woman, Fay was now an invalid in a wheelchair.

Like many others who suddenly find themselves incapacitated, Fay's greatest problem was that her mind wanted to do, but her body would not let her. Accustomed to caring for others in her church and her home in addition to being a very active substitute teacher, she now found herself dependent upon the very ones who had always counted on her.

Beneath the Peel

How did she make the adjustment? As Fay puts it, "Either you draw closer to God or you drift away from Him." She could have added a third possibility that is fairly common: "Or you blame Him for letting this happen to you."

Is everything that happens to us God's will? While this could be considered a deep theological question, perhaps the answer is to be found in response to another simpler question: *Is this heaven, or is it only earth?*

Jesus taught us to pray: "Your will be done, on earth as it is in heaven" (Matt. 6:10*b*). The implication is obvious: heaven is where God's will is the order of the day and earth is the place where God's will occasionally is done. That God's will does not reign supreme on earth is painfully obvious from the litany of society's evils that confront us each day—murder; theft; alcoholism; families torn apart by strife; wars; lives ruined by drugs, envy, or greed.

> **Read John 10:10. What does God want for us?**

A pastor's wife tearfully told of her rebellion against God for years. The reason? Her mother had died when she was quite young, and well-meaning Christians sought to comfort the little girl by telling her that her mother's death was God's will and she had to accept it as such. Her reaction? If God is so cruel that He takes a mother away from her children, then I want no part of Him. Only when she became a young woman did she learn through personal Bible study and the example of others not to blame God, Who loves us, with all the misfortunes that come our way. Only then could she enter into a personal relationship with her Redeemer.

The tragedy is that many people do not get beyond the initial bitterness they feel toward God when affliction strikes. Christians inadvertently contribute to this when they remind the victim that "it is God's will."

> **Read Job 19:6-10. How did Job react when told that his misfortune was the will of God?**

Yet, Job learned a great lesson: the true nature of God. His fuller knowledge of God led him not only to personal repentance

> **Read Job 42:1-9. What does Job say that God said to him?**
>
> **What does God say to Job's presumptuous friends?**

but to pray for those who had wronged him (Job 42:10). He learned that God is loving and forgiving, and he sought to make these characteristics his own.

Fay had been studying the Book of Job in her church just before her personal tragedy struck, and oftentimes during the months she lay in the hospital she reflected upon that study. She also pondered the suffering of Jesus on the cross, and found hers small by comparison. She realized she had not been singled out for punishment by God Who, after all, had

> **Read Matthew 5:45.**

warned us that the rain (and even tornado debris) falls on the just and the unjust; but she also knew the promise of Romans 8:28.

> **Read Romans 8:28. In your own words, what does this verse mean?**

Life had dealt her a lemon; she lost a leg, but she is determined to exchange that bitter fruit for one of a richer color, full of goodness. She is convinced that God has a purpose for her life.

When tragedy strikes, life changes not only for the victim but for the entire family. Charlene's very active life in her community and church came to an abrupt halt the day her husband fell from a ladder, paralyzing him from the waist down. Now, her life revolves around meeting his needs.

All too often, strife and hard feelings spill over as families struggle to deal with the new circumstances. All are busy, with full schedules, yet

> **Has your life been changed by tragedy? If so, how might the meaning of Romans 8:28 change how you view your circumstances?**

someone must become the caretaker. While old age is a blessing and not a tragedy, the care of the elderly is a dilemma that affects all families. Who will rearrange his or her (and it is usually her) life to meet the needs of the family member?

I will never forget the disbelieving expression on Carmen's (my friend in Spain) face as I shared news of my sister's wedding with her. She could not understand that she would marry. "Here," she explained to me, the new missionary, "the youngest girl in the family stays home to care for the parents." I thought of single women I had met in Spain and realized the truth of what she was saying. Today that tradition, along with many others, is being abandoned by a modern society, but even in our country the conviction persists that a single person can more easily become a caregiver. Married members of the family unfairly assume the single will accept this responsibility, often not appreciating the difficulties to be faced when the individual must also continue to work full time. Repressed resentment or open conflict can be the result.

Support from family and friends is crucial whether one is the sufferer or the caregiver. Both Fay and Charlene felt the strength gained from many prayers, and from the support of a giving church family.

Arthur Walker, who was interim pastor of the Baptist church in Brent that fateful May, remarked at the time: "I pray Brent Baptist will not be known for the tornado, but will be known for spreading the gospel and for reaching people."

What a goal for all who suffer afflictions! That others would see past the handicap and see the love of God shining. Tough high school students who had known Fay Dowdle as a substitute teacher explained why they visited her: "We can tell when people care for us."

> **If your life is affected by tragedy, write out how you would like to use your circumstances for the glory of God. If your life is not currently affected by tragedy, write a pledge to stop and consider how God might use you in the event of future tragedy.**

CHAPTER 7

For the Lonely

"It is not good that the man should be alone" (Gen. 2:18a).

The Bright Orange Skin

The shock reverberated throughout the academic community. A brilliant young professor in a leading state university had been found dead of carbon monoxide poisoning in her car. Those who worked alongside her and those who studied under her had a difficult time reconciling the irrefutable facts with the smiling, perky woman they knew—or thought they knew.

This tragedy reveals how often in today's world we know only the side someone chooses to reveal. Suicide rates and drug and alcohol addictions are indicators of the tremendous number of individuals adrift in a sea of loneliness.

How do we as Christians respond to loneliness—our own, first of all? We know the *right* answer: "My God is all-sufficient for me." Yet, we are sometimes like the child who was afraid of being left in a dark room at night. When his mother assured him he would not be alone, that God would be with him, the child responded, "Yes, but I want someone with a face." Our deep desire for the company of someone with a face is not an indication at all of a weak faith, but rather of our humanity.

That was my experience as a young missionary in language study. There was no evangelical church in the town where we lived, leaving us for the first time in our lives without the bolstering moral and spiritual support of a family of fellow believers. The one other American family we knew in the city left soon after we got to know them. I could barely speak enough Spanish to buy food. I was lonely. After being awash in tears of self-pity one day, God gave me an idea and an opportunity to test it.

One of our son's five-year-old classmates was hospitalized for a couple of months. Somehow, I was able to communicate to the mother that I would be happy to stay with Javier each morning after delivering our children to preschool and before my own classes began. So, each morning Javier patiently listened as I haltingly read stories to him and I listened as he sweetly corrected my worst mistakes. But the greatest personal benefit I received was that I was no longer lonely. In meeting the need of others, I fulfilled my deep need for companionship.

Since that discovery long ago, I have applied this formula countless times: when lonely, ask God to lead you to someone else who is lonely, too. So often this person is even lonelier than I, for she does not have the benefit of God's friendship. The fulfillment of physical, emotional needs becomes the open door for the beginning of a spiritual journey of faith for the new friend.

Beneath the Peel

Does the Bible speak to this aspect of our lives? Just ask Elijah as he challenged Ahab or as he sat under the juniper tree. Ask David and, yes, even ask Jesus.

> **Read 1 Kings 19:1-18. How did God respond to Elijah's loneliness?**

> **Read Psalm 25:16, then Psalm 30:11-12. Who is crying out in loneliness? How does God cheer him?**

Many times during His short journey on Earth, Jesus was alone. Being alone, however, is not the equivalent of being lonely. Jesus often sought solitude in order to commune with His Father, to reflect on His ministry, to focus, and to seek relief from the pressing demands of the crowds. As busy women in today's demanding society, we also have a need for solitude from time to time for the same reasons. Quiet moments can refresh the body and calm the spirit. Moments spent in communion with our Heavenly Father will bring us closer to Him and provide us with the inner strength so vital to living a meaningful life.

Loneliness can occur even in the midst of crowds. More than a physical situation, it is a sense of being forsaken. When Jesus was on the cross, He was truly lonely (Mark 15:34).

Yet, that abandonment experienced by the Son of Man was a temporary loneliness that resulted in the victory of God's eternal presence for all who would trust in Him.

> **Read Psalm 67:6. What does God give for the comfort of the lonely?**

God surrounds the solitary with family. But what about all those who no longer have the closeness of a family to sustain them—the widow and the widower, the grandparent who lives far from the grandchildren, the single adult who goes home each night to an empty house?

When she saw us arrive at the travel agency just after she locked the door, she very graciously reopened the office to sell us the plane tickets we needed for the next day. We thanked her for her willingness to work late that night only to hear her respond: "I don't have anything to go home to anyway, except a dirty apartment and a mountain of dirty clothes."

Countless women across our land could make the same or a similar statement. (Maybe their clothes are clean!) So many live alone—never married or alone after having lost a mate, either through death or divorce. Alternate refuges fill the void—work, TV, singles bar, alcohol—but they only cover up for a time rather than solve the need for intimate human relationships.

Loneliness, however, is not limited to the single. Even in a family, isolation and loneliness are often present. The tragedy is that we are so busy we may not notice.

There are so many *good* demands on our time! After work on Monday, there is grocery shopping to be done. Tuesday night, the Women on Mission prayer group meets. Wednesday night, we dash off to church supper, prayer service, and choir, but the children have their activities, too, so that's OK. Thursday night is either PTO, a committee meeting, or a shower for Joan down the street. A rare night at home is spent watching a movie. Busyness covers up the lack of intimacy, but it cannot be a substitute.

Loneliness is augmented if you are also without the presence of the God Who longs for your fellowship. He is ready to give you sustenance, to exchange your emptiness for a joyful song, and to celebrate with you a victorious life.

> **Read Romans 15:1-7. In this passage are several suggestions which might serve to alleviate the loneliness of another. List them below.**

God's church has a responsibility that goes beyond helping the lonely heart connect with its Creator. The church is to be the family for those who have none at hand. Caring enough to be there for others is a very important part of our ministry as a member of God's family. The human presence we offer will be more welcome than even a cold, juicy tangerine for the hot and weary traveler.

In ministering to the lonely, our loneliness disappears.

CHAPTER 8

For the Busy Mother

"Let the little children come to me, and do not stop them; for it is to such as these that the kingdom of heaven belongs" (Matt. 19:14).

The Bright Orange Skin

You have heard the lament before: "I was not prepared to be the mother of a teenager. I don't know if I will survive or not."

She voiced her frustration to a stranger as both waited in line at the post office. "You need to lock them in a closet when they turn 12 and not let them out until they are 21." Her listener responded: "That's probably too soon. I have a 21-year-old."

Motherhood! Is it being the cell-block guard who throws away the key, the angel described in honey-coated phrases on Mother's Day cards, or somewhere in between—perhaps a little of both? Is it the curse of a vengeful God (Gen. 1:16) or one of life's greatest blessings (Psalm 113:9)?

Your answer to that question is important, as your attitude

> Read Genesis 33:5 and Psalm 127:3-5. What do they say about children?

toward the state of motherhood will largely determine your reactions to its many demands.

The precious trust of having children is not one to be taken lightly. Study after study has shown that the strongest influence that children receive during their early, preschool years is that of the parent. At that tender age, children learn by imitation. The best gift that parents can give their child is the example and the memory of a home filled with love, where the husband and wife treat each other with respect and kindness. Open communication between all members of the family and a relationship based on honesty, forgiveness, and acceptance are essential to providing the type of stability that a child needs. The responsibility of the parents to teach by example is a frightening one as it demands a genuineness of life. How many times have teenagers been turned against God and His church by the contradictions they witness in the face their parents present in church and the one they see seven days a week at home!

Beneath the Peel

Have you ever eaten a tangerine with a lot of seeds? When we do, our enjoyment of the juicy fruit is diminished by the bothersome seeds. Not all that is beneath the peel is good and desirable. Love is like that. It can be delightful and beneficial to all concerned, or it can leave a bitter taste. Experiences show that it is as possible for love to do harm as it is for it to do good. The Bible includes some real-life examples of love that proved destructive.

It seems that Jacob himself had learned nothing of his own childhood when he was the favorite of his mother Rebekah while his father Isaac favored his twin Esau (Gen. 25).

Showing favoritism is only one of many ways to

> **Read Genesis 37. In what way was the love of Jacob for Joseph harmful?**

love incorrectly. Parents often make the mistake of confusing permissiveness with love. Not wanting to infringe on the development of their individuality, we hesitate to correct our children or to demand much of them. Too often, we seek to express our love through providing what money will buy, and we even exchange time without children for a salary in order to buy them the brand name shoes that are currently the status item. Sometimes mothers even make the mistake of smothering children with love, making them overdependent in order to satisfy a necessity the mother feels for being deeply needed by someone.

Yes, it is possible to make many mistakes in our attempts to express love for our children. If we wish to learn the correct way, we need to study the way in which God expresses His love for us.

> **Read Jeremiah 31:3, 1 John 4:8, John 3:16, and Romans 5:5,8. In what two ways does God express His love?**
>
> **Now read John 14:15. How does God expect us to respond to His love?**

> **Read Revelation 3:19. What is another component of parental love?**
>
> **What element of discipline is described in Hosea 11:1-4?**

In God's kind of discipline, there is no place for either physical or emotional abuse, rather for loving yet firm correction and even punishment when necessary. Proper discipline is an exercise in what is known today as "tough love."

Verses such as Deuteronomy 6:6-7 and Proverbs 22:6 remind us of another responsibility parents have.

It is too easy to leave these matters up to the church and/or the school, but God makes it evident in many places in His Word that parents should take seriously their own responsibility in the spiritual and moral training of their children.

> **What do Deuteronomy 6:6-7 and Proverbs 22:6 say about parental responsibility?**

In seeking to "train children in the right way" (Prov. 22:6), it is important to keep in mind that a child is an adult in formation. To enable that child to reach the ultimate goal—a mature, independent adult with a strong Christian faith—he must be given responsibilities commensurate with his capabilities. This includes the opportunity to make decisions and take initiatives within the bounds set by his parents. One of the freedoms God gives His children is the freedom to make mistakes, and parents should realize there can be no growth without errors along the way. Even King David admitted he had some problems growing up (Psalm 25:7), and he asked forgiveness for his rebellious ways. Parents will have many opportunities to forgive their children, and even to seek forgiveness from them, but children need to be taught that true repentance involves a sincere desire not to repeat the same old mistakes.

Mothers have always had a heavy load to carry. Great-grandmother surely did not have it easy boiling the clothes in the big black pot over the fire in the backyard! But, in the past, a woman's tasks were home-centered for the majority. This is no longer the case. Today, large numbers of women work outside as well as within the home. Many of these mothers provide the primary if not the only financial support for their family. Many face the additional challenge of being at least a part-time mother to another woman's children as blended families are emerging as the predominant family structure in the United States if present trends continue.

Surely the demands and the stresses mothers face are great. For that very reason, mothers need to reflect on what is truly important and what is just unnecessary clutter. Just as it becomes impossible to sit in a chair that is overloaded with too many discarded shirts, books, and pants, so does it become extremely difficult to function as an effective mother if we allow our lives to become too full of good-but-not-essential activities. And in that latter category, certain church activities can be included.

As mothers, we must reflect seriously on what God teaches us concerning our parental responsibilities and give them the importance that should be theirs. This proper alignment of priorities will give a freedom and a confidence to enjoy the blessings God gives us in children.

> **If you are a mother, take a few minutes to reflect on how you have raised or are raising your children, or even grandchildren. What might you do to improve the example you set? If you don't have children, think of ways that you can be involved in the lives of children at church or in your neighborhood. How might you be able to set an example as a mentor or teacher? Set some goals.**

CHAPTER 9

For the Rejected

"The Lord upholds all who are falling, and raises up all who are bowed down" (Psalm 145:14).

The Bright Orange Skin

"My husband, my friend . . .

If any were ever one, then surely we."

The delicately cross-stitched words hanging on the bedroom wall mock the reality. The union celebrated there was broken by divorce.

Through three long years of separation, the wife had prayed for reconciliation, but it had not come. She remains convinced divorce is contrary to God's will and to biblical teaching even as she struggles to refocus a life she never anticipated living alone.

Cynthia and her pastor-husband seemed the ideal couple to their congregation. Both were warm and outgoing, with a magnetism that drew others to them. Then, the impossible happened. Devastated by rejection by the man who had promised to love and cherish her forever, she felt deceived, humiliated, and a failure as a woman.

So did Mary, Jean, and Carol—all missionaries until divorce

ended their marriages and careers. Sue was a deacon's wife. That is, until he told her he had fallen in love with a young woman at the office.

More and more women who are earnest Christians find themselves labeled with a big "D"—divorced/discarded. There is no magic bubble that protects Christians from the ills of the society in which we live.

Beneath the Peel

How can two Christians come to the point in their marriage when divorce seems the only solution? Does prayer not work?

Yes, God hears our pleadings, and answers them when *we let Him*. That is the key. We must remember that He chose to grant each of us free will—the will to obey or the will to choose not to obey. Men and women continue to choose a way other than God's.

> **Read Genesis 3. What were the consequences of the choices made by these first humans?**

Just as God chose not to force us to be reconciled with Him, so He has chosen not to force us to reconcile with each other. The failure of Christian couples to resolve their differences before divorce is not a sign of God's failure, but rather an indication that one, or perhaps both, has chosen another way.

> **Read Malachi 2:16. How does God feel about divorce?**

God hates divorce. Yet, He permitted Moses to write a law governing divorce because of the hardness of heart of those who rejected God's plan for marriage to be a life commitment as two, man and woman, became "one flesh" (Gen. 2:24). The ripping away of a portion of one's flesh is always painful. Healing can be a slow process.

Are divorcées the only women who experience the pain of rejection? What of the countless women who struggle to maintain the outward signs of a conventional marriage, trying to hide the lack of love in their lives? What of the mother whose children find her bothersome, her presence embarrassing? Does not she, too, feel her usefulness in life is over? Or the career woman, cut out of a conversation by her peers or passed over for a promotion?

Rejection comes in many forms and in varying degrees, but it always hurts and causes us to question our value. In our success-oriented society, it can be devastating. It can make one feel about as useful as a rotten tangerine.

The large block of marble had been lying around for some 40 years. The sculptor had marred it so severely that no one could think of a useful purpose so it had been discarded, left to collect dust. Finally, in 1501, the Cathedral Board of Florence, Italy, decided to get it off their hands by offering it to another artist. Could he use the badly-damaged block?

Recognizing the flaws, yet seeing the potential, Michelangelo took up his chisel. Blow by blow, David emerged from the cold, hard stone and seemed to take on life. To this day, thousands endure long lines in Florence to marvel at the result, not aware or even caring that this had been a flawed piece of marble that was saved from destruction by the touch of a master.

Just as God sees a round, orange, nourishing tangerine in a tiny bud, He sees in each of us a potential that only the Creator can. He saw it in Peter, in spite of his having failed so many times. He saw it in a slave boy named Joseph and in the child Samuel. No matter what we are or have been, no matter how others regard us, God is aware of a great possibility that we ourselves ignore.

> **Read Jeremiah 18:1-10. What does this passage say about God's intention in creating us?**
>
> **How does this make you feel about yourself?**

Traveling with Tangerines

The potter had a plan in mind as his hands molded the clay spinning on his wheel. But, something went wrong. Perhaps his hand hit a pebble, or perhaps there was a hard, dry spot. Maybe his fingers slipped a little. Whatever happened, the pot did not turn out as he had planned. The potter faced a choice: toss out the clay—discard it—or change the plan slightly and reshape it into another useful pot.

Only when the clay is totally resistant to his will and touch can it not be formed by the potter. Our lives are like that clay. As long as we are willing to submit, God lovingly reshapes, remolds, begins afresh with each of us after we stumble along the path to His perfect plan. He is willing to take a broken, disheartened soul and give it a new purpose for living. That is what forgiveness and rebirth are all about.

Far from rejecting us, God gathers us into His arms with the assurance that, yes, my child, you can do it. You can overcome whatever defeat has temporarily knocked you down. You will be stronger and kinder, more understanding of others, because of your moment of pain. You will also find that the new song that floods your heart will be filled with a deeper joy.

> **Read Psalm 139—the entire passage. If you have ever been rejected, how does this make you feel? Can knowing that God knows you intimately and created you specifically change how you feel about rejection?**

CHAPTER 10

For the Blended Family

"Holy Father, protect them in your name . . . so that they may be one, as we are one" (John 17:11b).

The Bright Orange Skin

In the United States, the traditional family is rapidly giving way to the blended family—a family composed of a set of parents with children that are "yours, mine, and ours." These families, which compose about 46 percent of all marriages in America today, are basically of two types, each with its own set of challenges. One is the result of the remarriage of a widow, a widower, or perhaps both. The other is a remarriage after divorce. Some of the problems faced by these two types of blended families are common to both, but others are unique to the particular situation.

A challenge that begins even before the marriage is that of winning first the acceptance and then the love of the child or children involved. Studies show that stepchildren in a second marriage are very threatening to a marriage. It is estimated that as many as 60 percent of remarriages will end in divorce when children are involved.

Unfortunately, this was Susan's experience. When she first

married Bill, she and his small daughter, Marie, got along fine. Susan enjoyed having the little one around. Then, it seemed that whenever Marie came for her visit, Bill had other plans. He loaded all the fishing gear in the car to be off with the guys while Susan stayed at home to take care of his daughter. As this happened month after month, Susan felt she was nothing more than the baby-sitter. Slowly, resentment built up.

This feeling grew after Susan and Bill had children of their own. For some reason, Bill always seemed to favor his first child at the expense of Susan's. After Marie moved in with Bill and Susan, the situation worsened. Susan was expected to be a mother to Marie, but she felt she was never permitted to discipline her. Her decisions would inevitably be overruled by Bill. Susan said, "I was told I had authority, but whenever I tried to use it, I was wrong."

Perhaps the end would have been a happier one for all if Bill had been aware of his responsibility in fostering goodwill toward Marie's new stepmother. If he had given her the support she needed, she would have been elevated in Marie's eyes as well.

Cynthia gives another viewpoint, that of the child caught in the middle between two families. Her life had been torn apart when her mother left her father. He had been distraught at the end of his marriage, and she had tried her best to comfort him while still remaining close to her mother. He so obviously wanted to reconcile that Cynthia hoped the marriage would be healed. Then, after a number of years, he met Emma and they were married. Cynthia's mother insisted her daughter have nothing to do with her father and his new wife. She told Cynthia she would have to choose either her mother or her father, that she could no longer relate to both.

Parents, stepparents, and children are torn between conflicting loyalties. All the possible frictions of a traditional family are multiplied by two as relationships become much more complex. The child has to relate to two sets of parents and four sets of grandparents who often compete for his affection. In his youth and immaturity, he easily confuses generosity and leniency with true love, and soon becomes a master at playing one set of parents against the other.

The child, of course, is competing for affection, also. He may be envious of a stepmother for *stealing* his father's affection. He may see the stepmother as a usurper of his mother's rightful place. If there are half brothers and sisters, or if the stepmothers have children of her own, he may regard them as rivals for his father's affection.

Beneath the Peel

There are so many hurdles in the way of a warm, loving relationship! How can they be overcome?

> **First John 4:19 offers one suggestion. What does it say?**

Love tends to beget love, just as spitefulness and faultfinding inspire negative reactions. If we desire love, we are first to learn to love and to show that love by our actions.

But, what if the child is not all that lovable? What if he is plain obnoxious, or devoted to making your life miserable? We must remember that doubtlessly God does not find us so easy to love, either. Think of all the times we disappoint Him, or fail to be obedient! Yet, in all our unattractiveness, we are loved by the Creator of the universe. As His great love fills us, it will surely overflow to others, even to that difficult child who perhaps wishes we had never come into his life.

In the case of remarriage after divorce, there are many relationships other than that with the children that add stress to the new marriage. Like it or not, the stepmother has to deal with the biological mother, even though it may be in an indirect manner through her children. The rivalry there can be intense. There may be resentment, too, over the financial support the husband continues to give to his former wife. Supporting two families frequently causes a very real financial bind.

Although the complexities of blended families are often seen as a problem unique to modern society, an examination of the Bible reveals to us once more the truth of the maxim, "There is nothing new under the sun." Take the case of Jacob.

> **Read Genesis 29:1-30:24. List kinds of blended family problems you see in Jacob's life at this time. Also read Genesis 37. What other problems do you see in Jacob's blended family?**

While we recoil at the thought of such practices, are we not guilty of the same basic error? Do not children today often find themselves pawns in the battle for love between adults? Many an unloved woman thinks she can gain a man's affection if she will only bear his child. Our country is strewn with the wrecked lives of young women who have found, as did Leah, that love is not a certain result of pregnancy.

Although Rachel died giving birth to her second son, the rivalry between the two sisters did not end. It lived on in their children. Sibling envy is perhaps inevitable when one child has been pitted against another in parental strife, and certainly so when one is so obviously favored as was Joseph. In any household that seeks to combine children of different parents, the temptation to favor one's own is always present.

In the midst of a difficult family situation, we would do well to look again at the tangerine. Some of the ugliest on the outside yield the sweetest fruit. Even a family as torn by rivalry, envy, deceit, lying, rape, and murder as was Jacob's gave Joseph to Egypt and, through the Bible, to the world. Alone in a foreign land, he had the courage necessary to suffer for his faith. This is all the more surprising when we realize that his family was one as divided on spiritual matters as it was on others. While his father worshiped the one true God, his mother Rachel stole and carefully hid her father's household idols. Yet, there stood Joseph, a beacon for God in a pagan land.

The other sons did not turn out so badly either. Their old rivalries gave way to love, for their father and for each other. This love was so strong that Judah even offered to become a slave in order that Benjamin might remain free. Through the trials of the years, they learned to live together and to value each other. All the sons shared in the blessings of their father—the sons of the slaves as well as the sons of the wives. While no one would like to emulate Jacob's troubled household of half brothers and sisters and jealous wives, his family is proof that God can continue to work with us and through us even in the most difficult situations.

A couple attempting to blend two families into one needs to be aware of the difficulties they face in order to overcome them. Each can help by always being supportive of the other and by encouraging the children to treat the new parent with proper respect. Jealousies can be minimized by treating both sets of children as equal members of the family. All the suggestions for living together in a primary family are valid for stepfamilies as well. It may take more work and even more prayer, but blending can take place as two families become one.

> **Are you or is someone you know part of a blended family? What problems do you see? Read 1 Corinthians 13 as if for the first time. Apply these principles of true love to the problems you have noted.**

CHAPTER 11

For the Communicator

"Do not let unwholesome talk come out of your mouths, but only what is helpful for building others up according to their needs, that it may benefit those who listen" (Eph. 4:29).

The Bright Orange Skin

"In the same room, they both kept silence." With these words, Carlos Edmundo de Ory begins the sad story ("The Postal Package") of a married couple for whom silence had become an unacknowledged but powerful barrier. They lived in the same small room, but they did not share their lives. He lived in his world and she in hers. Communication between them had ended long ago, and silence—a menacing silence—now ruled their lives.

Marriage counselors reveal that the problem of this imaginary couple is all too real. Lack of communication is the number one marriage problem. Wives complain that their husbands do not listen to them and husbands complain that their wives do not understand anything they say.

What is communication? How can we know if we have truly communicated?

Communication is more than talking and listening, as necessary as they are. True communication involves comprehension.

This common understanding of meanings is not as easy to achieve as it may appear. Body language and tone of voice may contradict the words and send out a confused message.

The father is seated in front of the television set watching a football game. His son enters, and starts to talk to him about a problem, but the father keeps his eyes glued to the screen. He answers the child, but his attention is clearly elsewhere. The message he sends, albeit unintentionally, is that the child's problem is not very important to him. Then, as the child grows older, the father wonders why his son never talks with him.

Communication involves much more than words. Experts say that words only contribute seven percent of the total message, with voice tone and nonverbal communication contributing the rest.

Oftentimes, messages are sent by actions rather than words. If a child refuses to eat, what message is he sending? Is he simply not hungry? Is he feverish? Or is he trying to get the attention of an otherwise absent parent?

Gala was an expert at manipulation at age five. Her mother was striving to make a career and raise her daughters alone. Under a great deal of stress, she unwittingly passed that stress onto them. Gala's reaction was to demand more of her mother's time, and she knew that if she refused to eat, her mother would give her undivided attention to Gala as she tried one trick and then another to get food in her daughter's mouth. Gala was trying to say through her actions what she could not put into words.

Another important facet of communication is the filter factor. We each listen with a preconceived idea, a prior attitude, a mind that is cluttered with past experiences. All of these work to give us an interpretation of what we hear that may or may not be the interpretation the speaker intended. Our own sensitivity is a very important filter that leads to many misinterpretations.

There are also a number of barriers to proper communication, barriers that can be overcome with effort. One of these is the fear of intimate conversation, of putting yourself on the line, so to speak. The danger of rejection is always present. It seems easier to the shy person to simply back away and keep silent.

Perhaps the greatest barrier to communication today is the rushed lifestyle of so many. There simply is no time to stop and talk. We jokingly say that we communicate by leaving messages on each other's answering machines. The days of whiling away the hours in pleasant conversation on the back porch seem to have gone with the horse and buggy.

At times, efforts at conversation go nowhere because the two individuals, like the husband and wife in Ory's story, inhabit different worlds. Parents do not have a clue as to what their teenagers are trying to say, and too often do not even know how they pass their time. The husband can only talk of his work, and his wife does not understand at all what he does there.

If communication is to take place, each party must make a conscious effort to understand the other. Lives and interests must be intermingled so that viewpoints can be understood, even if not shared. We must care enough for another that we are willing to work at truly communicating with that person.

Beneath the Peel

The Bible has a good bit to say about the art of communication. The three basic steps—speaking, hearing, and understanding—can all be learned by studying and applying biblical principles.

> **Read Ephesians 4:25-26 and Colossians 3:8-9. What do these verses say about communication?**
>
> **What important principle is mentioned in both passages?**

The lack of truthfulness has led to the demise of many a marriage. When a wife states, "I can't believe anything he says," the marriage has already been seriously damaged. Trust depends upon truthfulness.

For the Communicator

> **What do Ephesians 4:29 and Romans 14:13 say about communication?**

Words are very powerful tools. They can be used to build or to destroy. One of the ancient Proverbs (19:13) compares a nagging woman to a dripping faucet. The Chinese realized the effect of such an annoyance when they incorporated slowly dripping water into their means of torture. The tension builds and builds until it becomes maddening.

Another way words can hurt is through gossip. Elizabeth oftentimes starts to tell something she has heard and then checks herself: "No, it will not edify." If words do not build up, more than likely they will tear down a person's reputation or, at least, cause doubts and suspicions. In such instances, it is best to leave them unsaid. It is easier to throw pamphlets from an airplane than to collect them later.

> **What does Proverbs 17:9 say about gossip?**

Being around Matt and Sally is quite an experience. A soft-spoken man, he will begin a conversation only to have Sally interrupt with a comment totally unrelated. He may keep talking, but her voice rises in volume until poor Matt is completely drowned out. But he is persistent. He has something he wants to say. Later, he will begin again, only to have the same scene repeated.

Sally controls the conversation. In the process, she annihilates her husband. It is evident from her comments that she has not even been aware he was speaking—or, if aware, that she gave no importance at all to what he said.

> **Read James 1:19-20.**

A good communicator doesn't seek to dominate the conversation.

Rather, a good communicator speaks simply and sensitively. She speaks personally, sharing her feelings. This requires some valor, because any time one reveals her feelings, she is making herself vulnerable. But if communication on a deeper level is sought, then one must be willing to take the risk and share on a deeper level.

Communication cannot take place without listening.

A good listener gives undivided attention to the one speaking. Careful listening lets the speaker know he or she is important to you.

> **Read John 13-17. Write down each instance in which the disciples heard what Jesus had to say through their own filters, adding their own interpretations.**
>
> **What did Christ do in John 16:17-30 to clarify what He was saying? When others misunderstood you, what can you do to improve communication?**

It is necessary for proper attention to be paid to the speaker if the listener is to pick up on subtle messages sent by body language and facial expressions. These were completely lost on the father who kept his eyes on the television.

A good listener is an active listener. She lets the other person know she is listening. This can be done by simply nodding the head, raising the eyebrows, or by verbal responses to what is being said. She makes an obvious effort to understand by asking pertinent questions. The repetition of what has just been said is another way of letting the speaker know you are giving him or her proper attention.

An important part of being an active listener is to look at the person speaking. This helps create an atmosphere of acceptance of the person, even though you may disagree with what is being said. Good listeners must fight against two common tendencies. The first is to exclude what we do not wish to hear (which usually does not agree with our preconceived idea). The second tendency that prevents proper understanding is that of "hearing" our interpretation of the message rather than what is actually being said. Developing the habit of active listening will help overcome both of these hindrances to communication.

Jesus made reference many times to the difference between hearing superficially and hearing with understanding (Mark 7:14). Indeed, one of the greatest problems He faced in His ministry was that of being misunderstood—each "heard" Jesus say what they wanted to hear rather than what He was truly saying.

We must realize that the possibility of being misunderstood depends as much upon the listener as the speaker. Seeking to apply some of the principles of good listening will aid in our efforts to properly understand others.

Good communication is not a panacea that will resolve all the interpersonal problems families face. It is possible to communicate well and still be divided by different values and goals in life. It is certain, however, that without open communication, personal intimacy is not attainable.

God Himself dared to communicate with humanity. His message is often misunderstood, and even rejected by the majority. His efforts to communicate with us were even costly, leading to the death of His Son on the cross. But, He refuses to give up. He keeps trying to get His message across. Those of us who accept what He is saying know the joy of vital communication with our Creator and Redeemer.

CHAPTER 12

For the Forgiven

"If you, O Lord, should mark iniquities, Lord, who could stand? But there is forgiveness with you" (Psalm 130:3-4a).

The Bright Orange Skin

She had not heard anything from her ex-husband since he left her and their two young daughters to fend for themselves eight years earlier. Being abandoned for another woman would have been difficult enough, but being abandoned for another man was so devastating to her that she was not able to even eat for some time. Her secure middle-class world of a young couple on the rise, joint owners of a growing business, two homes, with a live-in maid was exchanged for living in a small one-bedroom apartment in the city and a struggle to make ends meet, while trying and failing at various jobs. He had made no effort to get in touch with them, to inquire about their daughters, to send them a little money from time to time. It was as if he had ceased to exist.

Then his family called, and she made the long journey to his hospital room with her pastor at her side. Together, they looked on the drawn face of a man dying of AIDS. What would she say to the man who had destroyed her life and her dreams? The words would not come easily. She had difficulty even breathing as she stood in the same room with his lover and other homosexual friends. Yet, she longed to share with him the love and acceptance she had found with her Lord and she knew the beginning was allowing God to love him through her. The beginning was to do for him what God had done for her.

"I forgive you," she said.

Beneath the Peel

Forgiveness of grievous wrongs is not human. It is our nature to desire to see those who mistreat us experience what they justly deserve. When we are in the vice of hatred and self-pity, we cry out with David, "Consume them until they are no more" (Psalm 59:13b).

> Read Nahum 1:2, Deuteronomy 32:35, and Hebrews 10:30. What does the Bible say about vengeance?

Joseph certainly had just cause to hate his brothers. Not only had he experienced the taunting that was a part of their expression of jealousy, but this favorite, spoiled son found himself sold into slavery. He who had others at his bidding now had to obey the commands of others. Talk about a change in lifestyle! Insult was added to injury when he was falsely accused by Potiphar's wife and imprisoned as a result. No one was looking for this prisoner in a foreign land; his father had long since believed him dead. He seemed a young man without a future.

But while Joseph was there in the prison, the Lord was with him (Gen. 39:20-21). The Lord's presence transformed Joseph, just as He still changes people today.

> Years later, when his brothers finally got around to asking for forgiveness more out of fear than of true repentance, what did Joseph do? Read Genesis 50:15-21.

God was able to bring good and the salvation of many people out of a bad situation because Joseph was content to wait on the Lord to work things out. God's presence saved him from being a bitter man, consumed with the desire for vengeance for all the injustices he suffered, and allowed him to become a compassionate leader, a blessing to the nation to which he had been carried in bonds, as well as a blessing to the "nation" that had sold him into slavery.

> Read and think about Micah 7:18*a*.

God's loving willingness to forgive is evident all through the Bible, from Genesis to Revelation. References are numerous. But the example that speaks most eloquently is that of Christ Jesus as He was hanging by nail-pierced hands on the cross. Surrounded by those who were sneering at Him even as He died, He prayed: "Father, forgive them; for they do not know what they are doing" (Luke 23:34).

It is comforting to us sinners to know our God is ever-ready to forgive the wrongs we commit. But, accepting God's forgiveness exacts of us a similar willingness to forgive. Jesus intimated that such was a part of the nature of having received God's kind of forgiveness when in the Model Prayer He gave us He included the words: "And forgive us our debts, as we also have forgiven our debtors" (Matt. 6:12). His parable of the ungrateful servant (Matt. 18:23-35) made the teaching too clear to miss.

Perhaps the home is the greatest training ground for the learning of forgiveness. It may be as minor an offense as one toddler snatching a toy from the hands of another, but conflict certainly seems to be a part of family life. It was even present in the family of our Lord when His brothers at first opposed His abandoning the carpentry shop in order to become an itinerant preacher.

Then and throughout His ministry, Jesus taught us by example some basic principles of resolving conflicts. Mark 3:1-6 tells of an incident that angered Jesus, but He expressed that anger in a creative way. He restored usefulness to a withered hand.

> **What would happen to conflict in our families if we looked for creative, positive ways to express anger?**

We are told that the repression of anger only makes for an early heart attack, but there are basically two ways of "letting it all out." One is the most common: lash out at the other person. "What? You didn't take out the garbage like I told you to? Can't you ever do anything right?" Anger at the lack of obedience is easily transformed into an accusation of the person. In anger, we seek to destroy.

The other method of expressing anger is that used by Christ. He attacked the wrong while at the same time affirming the person. The case of the adulterous woman in John 8:1-11 is a good example of that. Jesus let her know that what she was doing was wrong, but He also expressed His faith that she would be able to change her way of living.

Let's go back to the garbage detail. Johnny still did not take it out, but how different the tone in the home would be if instead of shouting out a damaging accusation the mother responded with words reminiscent of Christ: "I am disappointed that you did not take out the garbage as I asked. Come take it out now. I'm sure that next time you will remember." Affirmation, not accusation, leads to the resolution of conflict.

This is possible only if the offending act itself is addressed rather than using the heat of the moment to bring up all the many failures of the child or the husband to live up to your standards. Someone overwhelmed with accusations will either fight back or withdraw into silence. Neither reaction will lead to solving the problem. In like manner, we must forget past offenses. That is where forgiveness comes in.

> **What does Paul admonish us to do in Colossians 3:13?**

There are times, too, when it is necessary for us to swallow our pride and ask for forgiveness. Sometimes this is necessary even when we are not aware of having committed a wrong, or when we are fully convinced of our innocence. Paul recognized this, and asked forgiveness of the church of Corinth for what he later realized had been a mistake (2 Cor. 12:13). The admittance of a possible personal error, however unintentional it might have been, is one of the characteristics of the new life in Christ. As the writer of Proverbs reminds us: "No one who conceals transgressions will prosper, but one who confesses and forsakes them will obtain mercy" (28:13).

The renouncement is an important part of that verse. It means, of course, that a conscious effort will be made not to repeat that same mistake.

Conflict is a natural part of life. If it is accepted as such, then we can move beyond the dead-end street of trying to determine blame and advance to the point of admitting there is a problem that needs solving.

Individuals react to problems and conflict differently, but it is a recognized rule that one person alone cannot resolve the conflict. There must be a willingness from all parties concerned. That is why unilateral talks never give the desired result on the international level. Professional mediators are customarily called upon to meet with representatives of the conflicting nations to work out a compromise.

Conflict on the home front, while on a much smaller scale, is often as impassioned as the conflicts that make the evening news, and is often more difficult to resolve because of its intensely personal nature. Yet, lessons can be learned from international diplomacy. Each side must give a little, accept compromise, and be determined that peace will be achieved.

As Christians, we are the "forgiven," and God's instructions to us are clear. "Put away from you all bitterness and wrath and anger and wrangling and slander, together with all malice, and be kind to one another, tenderhearted, forgiving one another, as God in Christ has forgiven you" (Eph. 4:31-32). Far from implying that we should pretend problems do not exist or that we should try to gloss them over in order to keep our halo in place, the Bible accepts the fact that conflict will exist and goes on to tell us how we should deal with it. Whether we are the cause or the victim is not the issue. In either case, there can be no doubt that God expects us to be the resolvers of conflict (Matt. 5:9). Forgiving and accepting forgiveness are to go hand in hand if we are to live as our Lord has shown us.

> **Is there someone you need to forgive? Do you need to seek forgiveness from another person?**

Tangerines for All

To the group leader: Use the following questions to guide discussion in a group study situation. Incorporate discussion of questions found throughout the chapters also.

Chapter 1
1. Why are people so hesitant to reveal they are being abused? What factors other than fear control such circumstances? How should the church minister to the abused? Should we become involved?
2. Realizing that children learn by both word and example, how can they be taught *not* to abuse others? What role does respect for others have in preventing abuse? Should Genesis 1:26 make a difference in the way we treat others?
3. How is your self-esteem? What does John 3:16 say of your worth? What does it say of the worth of others? Does it have anything to say to the problem of abuse?

Chapter 2
1. Carefully read Ecclesiastes 3:1-8. How can you relate the truth observed in verse 1 to this particular season in your life? Do you need to reorganize your priorities?
2. Do you think James 1:27 can relate to all single moms, regardless if they are truly widows or not? If so, what does that say to you as a Christian? What does that say to the church? Do you know any single moms who could use your help? How could you offer it in a nonoffensive way?
3. Read carefully Acts 18. How did Priscilla serve the Lord through her work? How can you more effectively use your career (inside or outside the home) to testify of your faith?

Chapter 3
1. What is the focus of your family? How does the family fit into "doing the Lord's work"? How do you minister as a family unit?

2. What are needs in your community that are going unmet? Can you change that? How would you go about it? Would it take time away from your family or could it become a family project?

3. Do you seek to apply Joel 1:3 personally, or do you depend on your church to take care of that responsibility? Are children learning by your example? In what ways?

Chapter 4
1. Grief can unite a family or it can tear it apart. What attitudes and actions contribute to each? How can destructive attitudes, such as attempting to fix blame, be avoided?

2. Any loss can result in grief. Other than death, what are some of these losses? Have you or someone you know suffered a loss that resulted in grief recently? How are you dealing with it? What place does God have in your or your friend's grief process?

3. Read John 15:26. Are you aware of the Comforter's presence in your life? How can you help His presence become a reality in the lives of others?

Chapter 5
1. The rich young ruler who spoke with Jesus was unable to give up his life of comfort for the uncertainties of following Jesus (Matt. 19:16-26). What about you? Which has first place in your life?

2. The parable recorded in Luke 12:41-48 is ultimately about relationships: the relationship of the owner to his property, between the owner and the steward, and of the steward with his boss's property. What application does this parable have to your life as steward of property that belongs to God?

3. What is your family's financial plan? What are your long-term goals? What are you doing now to reach them? Is there a joint effort, or strife caused by disagreement? How does your Christian faith relate to your money management?

Chapter 6
1. We spend our lives "growing up" to be independent. What lessons can we learn from being obliged to become dependent?

2. Fay received sustenance from Psalm 121:1-2. Do you live by those words? What difference does that realization make in your life? Does it result in nervousness or calmness in the face of difficulties?
3. Read the conversation Job had with Jehovah in chapters 38-42 of the Book of Job. Is it God's will that we suffer? What is the purpose of God for your life? Are you fulfilling this purpose? Are you willing to adjust to changing needs?

Chapter 7
1. Is being alone synonymous with being lonely? Reflect on Luke 6:12; 9:18 to explain your answer.
2. Am I afraid of intimacy—with God, with my family, with fellow Christians? How can I overcome that fear? How can I deepen my relationships? Does 1 John 4:11-21 speak to this problem?
3. As a Christian woman, what is my responsibility to the lonely? How can I become a friend to a lonely person?

Chapter 8
1. What does motherhood mean to you? Is the teaching of Proverbs 22:6 a part of your philosophy of parenting? How do you seek to put that verse into practice? Are you careful the idea you give your child of God is true to the teachings of the Bible?
2. Can you harm people by loving them? What causes a parent to show favoritism? To be permissive? To pamper?
3. Do you give your child the freedom he/she needs to mature in the image of Christ? How has the giving and receiving of forgiveness been a part of that maturation process?

Chapter 9
1. Do you agree with the opinion expressed in Proverbs 30:21-23? If you are that "unloved woman," what difference can the truth of Romans 8:35-39 make in your life?
2. Read carefully Jeremiah 18:1-4. Are you allowing the Lord to reshape you? Are you willing to leave your future in His hands?
3. Christ Himself was "the stone that the builders rejected" (1 Peter 2:7). He understands. Do we share that understanding, that

compassion for others? Who do you know who feels discarded? What can you do to accept and support that person?

Chapter 10
1. Meditate upon 1 John 4:19. What are some concrete ways you can show love to your stepchildren? Review the section on good/harmful ways to express love in the chapter "For the Busy Mother." Are all the ways you can show love positive ones? Can any of them be selfish on your part while actually working against the best interests of the child?
2. Why do you think God was able to bring good out of the divided and troubled family of Jacob? How can God bring good from your family situation? What adjustments will be necessary on your part? Will you need to change the way you relate to members of your household?
3. Could your community benefit from a support group for blended families? How could your church establish a ministry such as this?

Chapter 11
1. Would the application of the principle Paul sets forth in Ephesians 4:29 change the way you talk to your husband? To your children? Would it change the way you talk about people? How can you alter your conversation in a way that would better build up your child's self-esteem? Your husband's?
2. What are the three aspects of communication? Which do you consider most important? How do you propose to increase your ability in this area?
3. How would you rate communication within your family? Are there frequent misunderstandings? How do you think these could be prevented? List some positive steps you plan to take to improve communication with your family members and your friends.

Chapter 12
1. Read carefully Peter's instructions in 1 Peter 3:9. Think of a

specific situation in your family or among your friends where you can put this verse into practice. How can you reply with a blessing?

2. Is there a right and a wrong time to attempt to resolve conflict? Read Proverbs 15:1 and Proverbs 25:15 before answering. Think of examples in your personal experience.

3. Reread Ephesians 4:31-32. Is there some bitterness or anger in your life that needs addressing? How will you handle it?